FACE TO FACE WITH
GORILLAS

by Michael "Nick" Nichols
with Elizabeth Carney

NATIONAL GEOGRAPHIC

WASHINGTON, D.C.

Monkey on your back? How about a gorilla? Young Sophie holds on for a ride at a reserve in Gabon, Africa.

FACE TO FACE

This once-captive gorilla now thrives in the wilds of Bateke Plateau National Park in Gabon, Africa.

What would it be like to be part of a gorilla family? One special day, I came very close to finding out!

It all started when gorilla researcher Mike Fay called to tell me that a lowland gorilla was visiting his camp. Western lowland gorillas are the most common type of gorilla in Africa. But they are shy, so we don't know as much about lowland gorillas or have many photographs of them. Also, because they are hunted for meat, they usually avoid humans.

So it was pretty unusual to have a lone silverback gorilla visiting the research camp. And he wasn't a very polite guest, either! He would knock down banana trees, throw bamboo, and pound his chest with his fists. These displays looked fearsome, but violence probably wasn't his plan.

Ebobo, as they called him, was an adult male with no family group to care for. He needed a family and was searching for females. Ebobo was probably bored and lonely. He was looking for some company.

The gorilla would come about once a month, and that frightened some of the camp workers. They begged Fay to let them kill the gorilla. They thought Ebobo was dangerous and a threat. Fay told them not to harm Ebobo; that he wouldn't hurt them.

Fay asked me to come quickly if I wanted to photograph Ebobo. I traveled across Africa to the camp and waited for the gorilla's next visit.

Two months passed without a sign of Ebobo. Then one day I fell asleep on a picnic bench. I felt the slightest stirring, and when I woke, there was Ebobo sitting right beside me! I called for Fay, and we rushed to follow the gorilla into the forest. Ebobo angrily stomped around. He grunted, beat his

HOW TO GREET A GORILLA

Here's how you can let a male gorilla know you mean no harm:

- Don't look him in the eyes.
- Bow, make yourself small.
- Don't mess with the gorilla babies in his troop.

6

chest, and knocked down bushes. He wanted to show us that he was the boss here, but we refused to run away in fear.

Then the gorilla's behavior changed. He seemed to realize, "These guys are with me now." He led us deep into the forest, pausing from time to time so we could catch up. The jungle growth was thick with thorns and brush. Fay wasn't wearing shoes, and I barely had any film, but we followed Ebobo until dark. How could we turn back? We were running with a wild gorilla. He led us into his world.

With a glance over his shoulder, Ebobo checks to see that Mike Fay and I are keeping up. Adult western lowland gorillas often have red hair at the top of their heads.

MEET

THE GORILLA

Like a king in his kingdom, Titus feeds from a giant senecio tree. The 17-year-old silverback had recently taken control of a troop from another male.

Although it was fun to be a part of Ebobo's group for a day, he really needed a family of other gorillas. After our trip into the jungle, no one heard from Ebobo again for a long time. Then, two years later, Ebobo surprised the camp with a return visit. And this time he wasn't alone. Two females were with him. Ebobo had found a family!

Gorillas are very social animals. They live in family groups, also called troops, which usually have about five to ten members, but I've seen them

 With playful energy to spare, young gorillas spend much more time climbing trees than adults do. Mountain gorillas like this one have longer hair than other types of gorillas.

as large as 30. A strong, experienced male called a silverback leads each troop. You can also tell a silverback by his hefty size and gray-haired back.

Gorillas are the largest of all primates—a group of animals that includes monkeys, chimpanzees, and humans. Although they're very strong, gorillas are peaceful, plant-eating animals. In fact, their favorite activities are eating and napping.

Each day, the silverback leads the troop through the forest in search of prime snacking spots. Gorillas eat plants, so food is usually plentiful. They munch on leaves, stems, fruits, seeds, and roots. An adult male can eat up to 60 pounds (27 kg) of food a day!

While the troop's adults take their daily nap, young gorillas often have playtime. Youngsters wrestle and chase each other across the jungle floor. To learn important survival skills, like how to find food, young gorillas watch and copy their mothers.

Baby gorillas stay with their mothers until they are four to six years old. Then they either take their place in the family group or go off in search of a group of their own.

Gorillas' lives sound pretty laid back, but danger is always lurking in the jungle. In tropical African

← *This map shows where the different kinds of gorillas can be found in Africa today.*

↓ *A baby western lowland gorilla rides on its mom's back while she feeds on swamp plants.*

HOW TO PLAY LIKE A GORILLA

- Climb trees.
- Swing on ropes and pretend they're vines.
- Giggle with your friends.
- Get a piggyback ride on your parent's back.
- Bend over and touch your knuckles to the ground. Now, knuckle walk like a gorilla.

forests, leopards prey upon young gorillas. Other males sometimes challenge silverbacks and try to take over their families. These rival males have even been known to kill the baby gorillas. It's the silverback's job to keep the family safe, which is partly why male gorillas are twice the size of females.

Ziz was a silverback from the Virunga Mountains who was great at this job. Ziz's family grew large while he was in charge. I followed Ziz to photograph his troop, and over time he came to know me.

One day the gorillas became uneasy. Ziz called all the babies to him and gathered them under his massive body. He stood in front of the females and sent the males into the surrounding area.

I wondered what Ziz was up to. Later I heard that a pack of wild dogs had come into the forest. But the dogs would have to go hungry that day—the gorillas were safe under Ziz's watch.

Ear-piercing hoots and chest beats are how silverbacks announce their arrival.

A GREAT APE

A silverback mountain gorilla huddles in the rain. Gorillas are the largest of the great apes. Males can weigh as much as 485 pounds (220 kg) in the wild.

Gorillas are one of our closest relatives. When I look into a gorilla's eyes, I feel a connection.

Gorillas fall into a group of primates called great apes. The group includes chimpanzees, bonobos, and orangutans. Great apes and humans have a common ancestor who lived long ago. About five to eight million years ago, scientists think humans and apes began to change into different forms. Today, humans and gorillas still have many traits in common. We are closely related in our physical forms and biology.

15

Great apes are also complex thinkers. They can use tools and communicate with language. A few captive gorillas have even been taught American Sign Language.

Except for orangutans, all great apes live in Africa. The three most common types of gorillas—western lowland, eastern lowland, and mountain—live in the central part of the African continent. The shaggy-haired mountain gorilla lives in a sliver of forests atop the Virunga Mountains on the border of Rwanda, Uganda, and the Democratic Republic of the Congo (DRC). Eastern lowland gorillas are found mostly in the DRC. Western lowland gorillas are the most plentiful, but their thick rain forest homes make them hard to count. New research shows there may be

▼ Apes and humans evolved from a common ancestor and share a similar body structure. But different species developed different adaptations to help them survive in their environments. Apes and monkeys walk upright for short periods, but humans are the only primate to walk upright consistently.

Orangutan

Bonobo

Chimpanzee

Gorilla

Human

⬆ *Between feeding stops, infants ride their mothers' backs. Young gorillas stay with their mothers for four to six years.*

more western lowland gorillas than we thought. As many as 250,000 may be living in west-central Africa.

All gorillas are endangered, but some are in more trouble than others. Scientists think certain kinds of gorillas could become extinct in the next 50 years. For them, being a great ape isn't always so great.

17

GIANT

My son Ian grew up in Rwanda, but he wasn't able to see a wild gorilla then because he was too young. Now that he is older, he has taken up the challenge of photographing, and helping to protect, gorillas.

CHALLENGES

A noisy charge through the jungle might scare off this silverback's rivals.

Our connection with gorillas is beautiful to see. A young gorilla—chilled by a cold rain—once crept under my friend's poncho. People can be so happy to see a wild gorilla that they are speechless.

But being closely related to humans comes with a cost: Gorillas can catch many of the same diseases we do. In fact, baby gorillas in zoos are given the same vaccines as human babies. A deadly disease called ebola can infect primates and humans, and

→ *A Congo stand illegally sells gorilla hands. Some people still believe that the hands give the ape's power to humans.*

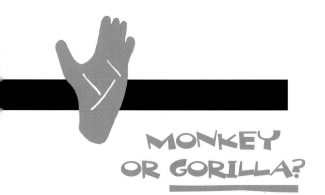

MONKEY OR GORILLA?

Can you tell the difference between a great ape and a monkey? If you're a gorilla, you:

— are larger than a monkey.

— have no tail.

— tend to knuckle walk on the ground rather than swing through the trees.

— have sharp vision and a short, broad nose.

there is no known cure. So far it has killed thousands of gorillas. Ebola often wipes out 95 percent of the gorillas in areas where an outbreak occurs. Over the past 25 years, threats like this have greatly reduced the population of western lowland gorillas.

The apes face other challenges too. Poachers sell gorilla body parts, which some people think are like magic charms and will make a human more powerful. Gorillas are also illegally hunted for meat.

Hunters sell the bushmeat in markets. Young gorillas whose mothers are killed will starve if they aren't rescued by conservation groups.

Habitat loss is an even bigger problem. Gorillas can't survive if their forest homes are cut down. Loggers chop down large areas to sell wood. Forests are sometimes cleared to make room for refugees, people who are forced to leave their countries. Without forests, gorillas have no source

⬆ Rwandan refugees carry firewood from the cleared outskirts of a national park that is home to mountain gorillas. Habitat destruction is one of the main threats to gorillas.

↑ *Visitors are too close to the apes at a mountain gorilla tourism program in Zaire, a country now known as the Democratic Republic of the Congo (DRC).*

of food or protection from predators.

Fortunately, many people are on the gorillas' side. Scientists are working on a vaccine to protect gorillas against ebola. New national parks protect gorillas from hunting and habitat loss.

Gorilla tourism has raised awareness and changed attitudes toward gorillas. Many people once feared gorillas and thought they were aggressive.

In the 1970s, a gorilla tourism program was begun in Rwanda. Visitors could see the animals in the wild. The program made a lot of money and helped people appreciate the animals. Gorillas' pictures were even printed on the country's money. Gorilla tourism spread to other African countries too.

Experts developed rules to keep both the tourists and gorillas safe. Tourists could only view gorillas that were used to humans. They also had to stay about 15 feet (4.5 m) from the animals. This was for both the gorillas' and the tourists' safety.

In the early 1990s, I pretended to be a tourist in what was then Zaire (now called the DRC) for a story I was doing. I went undercover to see if these rules were being followed. They were not. Tourists

This rescued orphan gorilla soaks up attention from a sanctuary employee. In time, human contact is stopped, and the orphans learn to function in gorilla society. They can then be released into the wild.

It's up to us to make sure gorillas have a future.

were allowed to stand just steps away from gorillas.

The tour guide led us to a big silverback. He weighed about 400 pounds (181 kg). I stepped away from the group to get a picture of them with the gorilla. Suddenly, I realized I was in trouble. The gorilla didn't like my movement. He pounded the ground with his fists and stood in an aggressive pose.

I knew I could not run faster than the gorilla, so instead, I looked down and fell to my knees. By making myself smaller, it was like I was telling the gorilla, "I know that you're the boss." The gorilla got the message. He turned and walked away.

Right away, the park rangers knew I wasn't just a tourist, because I knew how to "speak" the gorilla's language. But the Zaire story I did helped make gorilla tourism safer for people and apes.

Since then, my son Ian Nichols has become a National Geographic wildlife photographer. Now it's his turn to inspire a new generation of conservationists and researchers, so we can always run with the gorillas.

HOW YOU CAN HELP

⬇ *A mountain gorilla mother holds on to her two-year-old.*

Gorillas touch the lives of everyone who studies them, visits them, and protects them. They need our help to avoid extinction. You can make a difference by learning all you can about gorillas and sharing what you know with your friends and family. Support gorilla conservation and visit gorillas in zoos to learn about them.

Many American zoos have cell phone recycling programs that can actually help gorillas' survival. Cell phones include a metal ore called coltan (columbite-tantalite), which is mined in central Africa. Booming cell phone sales have led to a big increase in coltan mining. The result: Gorilla habitat has been dramatically reduced. Recycling phones cuts down the need for more coltan.

Since many gorilla populations are located in countries suffering from war and unrest, conservation efforts are complicated. For example, some very dedicated park rangers are fighting to protect mountain gorillas that live within the Democratic Republic of the Congo. These rangers put themselves in great danger to help the gorillas. Over the past decade, the forests of Virunga National Park have been illegally logged to produce charcoal. Civil war, in the country and outside of it, created many refugees, which made it hard for the government to protect the land. Rebel forces cut down forests. During this time, 120 park rangers were killed in clashes with the rebels. Now gorillas themselves have become a target. A number have been needlessly killed.

The conservation group WildlifeDirect supports Virunga National Park rangers and helps them keep themselves and the gorillas safe. You can help by raising money for conservation organizations like WildlifeDirect, the International Gorilla Conservation Program, the Wildlife Conservation Society, and the Dian Fossey Gorilla Fund. Your teachers might help you organize a book sale at school, or you could ask your parents to have a yard sale.

IT'S YOUR TURN

Not everyone has the opportunity to travel all the way to Africa to see gorillas firsthand. Fortunately, several zoos around the United States have gorilla exhibits where you can get face to face with the great apes.

The Bronx Zoo in New York City has the world's biggest manmade African rain forest. Their Congo Gorilla Forest is home to 22 lowland gorillas divided into two troops. The gorillas have large outdoor and indoor habitats that are filled with hundreds of species, including some African plants that had never been grown in New York before. The exhibit's creators didn't want the space to be just a great home for gorillas. They hope it inspires humans to take a greater interest in them.

How would you build a gorilla habitat? Now that you know how gorillas live in the wild, pretend you're a zoo director with plans to build a gorilla exhibit. What will your gorillas need to be happy and healthy in captivity? What are some ways you can teach zoo visitors about gorillas? How can you make more zoo visitors take an interest in gorilla conservation?

⬇ Orphan gorilla Makwa plays with a staff member at a Congo gorilla sanctuary.

FACTS AT A GLANCE

⬇ *Gorillas usually get around on all fours by knuckle-walking. They fold their short, thick fingers back and support part of their weight on their knuckles.*

▰ Scientific Name

There are two gorilla species, *Gorilla gorilla* and *Gorilla beringei*. These include the western lowland gorilla, which scientists call *Gorilla gorilla gorilla*; the Cross River gorilla, *Gorilla gorilla diehli*; the eastern lowland gorilla, *Gorilla beringei graueri;* and the mountain gorilla, *Gorilla beringei beringei*. Gorillas belong to the family Hominidae, along with humans, and to the order Primates, along with humans, chimpanzees, orangutans, and monkeys.

▰ Size

The average weight of adult male gorillas in the wild is 370 pounds (180 kg), and they stand about 5.5 feet tall (1.75 meters). Gorillas in zoos are often a little heavier—one captive male weighed 605 pounds (275 kg)! Male gorillas are ten times stronger than the biggest football players. Females are a lot smaller. They are about half the size of males.

▰ Lifespan

In the wild, gorillas live 35-40 years, but in captivity they have been known to live 50 years. Life as a baby gorilla is tough, though—about half of them don't survive infancy.

▰ Behavior

Gorillas make nests to rest in during the day and sleep in at night. To build a nest, a gorilla sits down and pulls branches and leaves around its body. Babies nest with their mothers. The silverback in a troop often babysits the youngsters while their mothers nap or forage for food. Older males nest on the ground, but females and younger gorillas sometimes build a nest in a tree. Scientists sometimes try to guess how many gorillas live in a particular area by counting the number of nests they find.

Gorillas are very social, and they like to groom one another. They make a sound like a giggle when they are having fun or being tickled.

Habitat and Range

Gorillas live in lowland tropical forests in central Africa. They live in parts of Cameroon, Central African Republic, Equatorial Guinea, Gabon, Nigeria, Republic of Congo, Angola, and the Democratic Republic of Congo (DRC). Mountain gorillas live at higher altitudes.

The area in which an animal lives is called a range. A western gorilla group needs a range of at least 7 square miles (20 km^2) to have enough food. Gorillas are not territorial. One group's range can overlap with another's.

Food

Gorillas eat over 100 different species of plants. They eat juicy stems, leaves, berries, fruit, vines, and even tear the bark off some trees. They also eat ants and termites.

Reproduction

Like humans, gorilla females are pregnant for about nine months before they give birth to a baby. A newborn gorilla weighs only four or five pounds, smaller than a baby human. The young gorilla will stay with its mother for three or four years. During this time it learns how to find food, escape from predators, build sleeping nests, and interact with other gorillas. Like humans, gorilla babies drink milk from their mothers. A female gorilla usually has her first baby when she is around ten years old, and has a baby about every four years. A male gorilla usually breeds when he is around 12 to 15 years old— when he has a troop of his own.

Biggest Threats

Loss of habitat is one of the biggest threats to gorillas' survival. Their habitats are destroyed for logging, mining, and building refugee camps. Other major threats are hunting and the ebola virus. Their best hope for survival in the wild is wildlife tourism programs. These programs bring money and jobs as guides to the local people, giving them reasons to take care of the gorillas.

A young orphaned gorilla plays on a vine in Gabon, Africa, on the Mpassa Reserve.

GLOSSARY

Endangered: A species with very few individuals remaining. If the number of individuals rises, the classification may change to "threatened" or "recovered." If the number falls, the species may become "extinct," meaning no individuals are left.

Forage: To search for food.

Habitat: The local environment in which an animal lives.

Poacher: A person who takes or kills an animal illegally. Poachers will sometimes kill gorillas and sell their meat or body parts; gorilla babies may be abandoned or sold as pets.

Primate: An order of mammals having large brains, forward-facing eyes, and opposable thumbs. An opposable thumb lets an animal grasp things, such as tools.

Range: The area in which an animal lives.

Silverback: An adult male gorilla who is the leader of his troop. He is called this because the hair on his back turns silvery white as he gets older.

Species: A group of animals or plants that look similar, can breed with one another, and have offspring who can also breed successfully.

Vaccine: A shot that can help prevent a person or animal from catching a disease like measles.

FIND OUT MORE

Books & Articles
Fowler, Allan. *Gentle Gorillas and Other Apes.* Children's Press, Inc., 1994.

Jenkins, Mark; photos by Ian Nichols. "In the Presence of Giants," *National Geographic* magazine, January 2008.

Nichols, Michael. *The Great Apes.* National Geographic Society, 1993.

Nichols, Michael, and Mike Fay. *The Last Place on Earth.* National Geographic Society, 2005.

Schlein, Miriam. *Jane Goodall's Animal World: Gorillas.* New York: Macmillan, 1990.

Films
Gorillas in the Mist: The Story of Dian Fossey. Guber-Peters Co./ Universal, 1998. Rated PG13.

Web Sites
www.wildlifeconservationfilms.com Take a virtual tour of the Bronx Zoo's Congo Gorilla Forest (and play the Conservation Quest Online Game) at http://www.congo gorillaforest.com/congohome.

Take a gorilla quiz, send an e-card, and play gorilla games at The Dian Fossey Gorilla Fund International, http://www.gorillafund.org/gorilla_fun.

This organization helps protect wild gorillas and their habitat.

Listen to a gorilla at the San Diego Zoo's Web site at http://www. sandiegozoo.org/animalbytes/t gorilla.html.

National Geographic Animal pages at http://animals.nationalgeographic .com/animals/mammals. Go to the Animals A-Z list, click on the letter G, and scroll to Gorilla, Lowland; and Gorilla, Mountain.

INDEX

Boldface *indicates illustrations.*

RESEARCH & PHOTOGRAPHIC NOTES

I use Canon cameras, and all my gorilla images were taken with film. If I were a young man at the dawn of my career, I would have loved to photograph gorillas with a digital camera. Digital cameras are capable of producing high-quality photos in low-light environments, which is where you commonly find gorillas. Plus, the contrast range is more suitable for capturing images of these black animals in their green settings.

My son Ian Nichols is part of this technological revolution in photography. When Ian was six years old, we lived at the base of Volcanoes National Park in Rwanda. I was working on my first book on mountain gorillas, while Ian attended the local school. There, his fascination with apes was kindled, but he wasn't old enough to see the wild gorillas himself.

After high school, Ian went to Gabon, Africa, to volunteer to work with orphan gorillas. Upon graduation from college in 2005, Ian received a National Geographic Society Young Explorers Grant to photograph chimps at a research site in the Democratic Republic of the Congo. The experience led to an assignment with *National Geographic* magazine to photograph western lowland gorillas. Ian's first story was published in January 2008. It features the first intimate images of a lowland gorilla group.

I've always wanted my work to be more than simply wildlife photography. I want it to incite action—I have a mission! When I chronicled Mike Fay's 2,000-mile trek across Congo and Gabon, he and I hoped to raise awareness about the habitat and perhaps spur the creation of a national park to protect the wildlife. The journey resulted in several articles, two books, and 13 national parks!

Ian's work now carries the same sense of purpose. He is a member of the International League of Conservation Photographers. He and his peers are the new vanguard of journalists who will inspire action by capturing the beauty of our natural world.   —MN

TO THE PARK GUARDS OF THE VIRUNGA VOLCANOES AND TO LIZ PEARSON ... PEOPLE WHO GIVE THEIR LIVES IN DIFFERENT WAYS TO PROTECT AND NURTURE GORILLAS. —MN

FOR MY GRANDMA DEE DEE, THE MATRIARCH OF OUR TROOP.—EC

Acknowledgments
I would like to express my deep gratitude to Meredith Montague for keeping me on track, and to my family Reba Peck and Ian and Eli ... and to the gorilla who taught me the most about family.

The publisher gratefully acknowledges the assistance of Christine Kiel, K-3 curriculum and reading consultant; and Craig Sholley (Senior Director of Development, African Wildlife Foundation) and Lisa Stevens (Curator, Primates and Pandas, National Zoological Park) for reviewing the text and map.

Photographs pages 11, 15, 18 by Ian Nichols; photograph page 19 by Kathryn Jeffery
Back cover photograph by Peter Wilkins

Book design by David M. Seager. The body text of the book is set in ITC Century. The display text is set in Knockout and Party Noid.

Front cover: Face to face with a western lowland gorilla in the Congo.

Front flap: This orphaned baby gorilla in Africa has a lot to learn before he can be returned to the wild.

Page one: A western lowland gorilla in Gabon, Africa, takes the easy way down.

Published by the
National Geographic Society

John M. Fahey, Jr., *President and Chief Executive Officer*

Gilbert M. Grosvenor, *Chairman of the Board*

Tim T. Kelly, *President, Global Media Group*

John Q. Griffin *President, Publishing*

Nina D. Hoffman, *Executive Vice President; President, Book Publishing Group*

Staff for This Book

Nancy Laties Feresten, *Vice President, Editor-in-Chief of Children's Books*

Bea Jackson, *Design and Illustrations Director, Children's Books*

Amy Shields, *Executive Editor*

Jennifer Emmett, Mary Beth Oelkers-Keegan, *Project Editors*

David M. Seager, *Art Director*

Lori Epstein, *Illustrations Editor*

Jocelyn G. Lindsay, *Researcher*

Carl Mehler, *Director of Maps*

Felita Vereen-Mills, *Senior Administrative Assistant*

Jennifer Thornton, *Managing Editor*

Grace Hill, *Associate Managing Editor*

R. Gary Colbert, *Production Director*

Lewis R. Bassford, *Production Manager*

Rachel Faulise, Nicole Elliott, *Manufacturing Managers*

Susan Borke, *Legal and Business Affairs*

Library of Congress Cataloging-in-Publication Data

Nichols, Michael.
  Face to face with gorillas / by Michael Nichols.
     p. cm.
  Includes bibliographical references and index.
  ISBN 978-1-4263-0406-4 (hardcover : alk. paper) -- ISBN 978-1-4263-0407-1 (library binding : alk. paper)
  1. Gorilla--Juvenile literature. I. Title.

QL737.P96N525 2009
598.3'3--dc22

2008023002

Founded in 1888, the National Geographic Society is one of the largest nonprofit scientific and educational organizations in the world. It reaches more than 285 million people worldwide each month through its official journal, NATIONAL GEOGRAPHIC, and its four other magazines; the National Geographic Channel; television documentaries; radio programs; films; books; videos and DVDs; maps; and interactive media. National Geographic has funded more than 8,000 scientific research projects and supports an education program combating geographic illiteracy.

For more information, please call 1-800-NGS LINE (647-5463) or write to the following address:

National Geographic Society
1145 17th Street N.W.
Washington, D.C. 20036-4688 U.S.A.

Visit us online at
www.nationalgeographic.com/books.

Librarians and teachers, visit us at www.ngchildrensbooks.com. Kids and parents, visit us at kids.nationalgeographic.com.

For information about special discounts for bulk purchases, please contact National Geographic Books Special Sales: ngspecsales@ngs.org. For rights or permissions inquiries, please contact National Geographic Books Subsidiary Rights: ngbookrights@ngs.org.

Printed in China